200 Last Verses for Manuals

Noel Rawsthorne

kevin
mayhew

kevin
mayhew

First published in Great Britain in 1998 by Kevin Mayhew Ltd
Buxhall, Stowmarket, Suffolk IP14 3BW
Tel: +44 (0) 1449 737978 Fax: +44 (0) 1449 737834
E-mail: info@kevinmayhewltd.com

www.kevinmayhew.com

This edition © Copyright 2009 Kevin Mayhew Ltd

The music in this book is protected by copyright and may not be reproduced
in any way for sale or private use without the consent of the copyright owner.

9 8 7 6 5 4 3 2 1 0

ISBN 978 1 84003 087 7
ISMN M 57004 153 4
Catalogue No. 1400161

Cover design: Rob Mortonson
Music setter: Sarah Stirling
Proofreader: Marian Hellen

Printed and bound in Great Britain

Foreword

Erik Routley, the famous church musician and scholar, has written that last verse harmonies must be done with 'restrained excellence, and without any sign of the congregation being thrown off course'.*

Others may judge the excellence or otherwise of the offerings in *Two Hundred Last Verses* but I do claim restraint for them, and many years as an organist have taught me how to encourage a congregation to enjoy hymn singing rather than to throw them off course. Last verse harmonisation is a tested and authentic part of our worship.

In *Two Hundred Last Verses* I have retained much of the original harmonic scheme while exploring new harmonic possibilities when going round a musical 'corner'. The result is often an unexpected and exciting modulation.

A sense of phrasing is the life-blood of music, and I have phrased all the hymns in order to encourage fine legato playing which will help the congregation give the words their full meaning.

Because of the chromatic nature of these arrangements, I have included a reminder that accidentals apply only to the bar in which they appear, and only at that pitch.

I have taken the opportunity provided by this revised edition to match the often lower keys found in the more recent major hymn books, while retaining those that are suited to older collections. In just three instances *(O filii et filiae, St Theodulph* and *Wiltshire)* it has been necessary to include two versions of the same tune, as the settings differ.

I do hope you enjoy playing these *Two Hundred Last Verses* as much as I have enjoyed writing them!

NOEL RAWSTHORNE

* *Words, Music and the Church*, Erik Routley (Herbert Jenkins, London 1969)

Contents

	No.		No.
Abbot's Leigh	1	Cross of Jesus	34
Aberystwyth	2	Crüger	35
Abridge	3	Culbach	36
Adeste fideles	4	Cwm Rhondda	37
All for Jesus	5	Darwall's 148th	38
All Saints	6	Deus, tuorum militum	39
All things bright and beautiful	7	Diademata	40
Amen Court	8	Dix	41
Angel voices	9	Dominus regit me	42
Angels' Song	*168*	Down Ampney	43
Anima Christi	10	Duke Street	44
Ar hyd y nos	11	Dundee	45
Aurelia	12	Easter hymn	46
Aus der Tiefe (Heinlein)	13	Ein' feste Burg	47
Austria	14	Eisenach (Mach's mit mir Gott)	48
Ave virgo virginum	15	Ellacombe	49
Away in a manger	*30*	Ellers	50
Billing	16	Es ist ein' Ros' entsprungen	51
Binchester	17	Evelyns	52
Bishopthorpe	18	Eventide	53
Blaenwern	19	Ewing	54
Bow Brickhill	20	Farley Castle	55
Bristol	21	Forest Green	56
Brother James' Air	22	Franconia	57
Buckland	23	Fulda	58
Bunessan	24	Gelob't sei Gott (Vulpius)	59
Caithness	25	Gerontius	60
Capetown	26	God rest you merry	61
Carlisle	27	Gonfalon Royal	62
Caswall	28	Gopsal	63
Contemplation	29	Greensleeves	64
Cradle song (Away in a manger)	30	Gwalchmai	65
Cranham	31	Hanover	66
Crimond	32	Harewood	67
Croft's 136th	33	*Heinlein*	*13*

	No.		No.
Helmsley	68	Morning hymn	104
Hereford	69	Morning light	105
Herongate	70	Moscow	106
Highwood	71	Mount Ephraim	107
Hollingside	72	Narenza	108
Horsley	73	Nativity	109
Hyfrydol	74	Neander (Unser Herrscher)	110
Irby	75	Nicaea	111
Irish	76	Noel	112
Kilmarnock	77	Noel nouvelet	113
King's Lynn	78	Nun danket	114
Kingsfold	79	Obiit	115
Lasst uns erfreuen	80	Offertorium	116
Laudate Dominum	81	O filii et filiae	117
Laudes Domini	82	Old 100th	118
Laus Deo (Redhead No. 46)	83	Old 104th	119
Leoni	84	Old 120th	120
Little Cornard	85	Oriel	121
Llanfair	86	Paderborn	122
Lobe den Herren	87	Passion chorale	123
Love divine	88	Personent Hodie (Theodoric)	124
Love unknown	89	Petra (Redhead No. 76)	125
Luckington	90	Picardy	126
Lux eoi	91	Praise, my soul	127
Maccabaeus	92	Puer nobis nascitur	128
Mach's mit mir Gott	*48*	Quam dilecta	129
Mannheim	93	Quem pastores	130
Marching	94	Ratisbon	131
Martyrdom	95	Ravenshaw	132
Melcombe	96	*Redhead No. 46*	*83*
Melita	97	*Redhead No. 76*	*125*
Mendelssohn	98	Regent Square	133
Merton	99	Repton	134
Michael	100	Rex gloriae	135
Miles Lane	101	Rhuddlan	136
Monkland	102	Richmond	137
Monks Gate	103	Rockingham	138

	No.		No.
Royal Oak	139	Surrey	175
Saffron Walden	140	Sussex carol	176
St Anne	141	Tallis' canon	177
St Bernard	142	Tallis' ordinal	178
St Clement	143	The first Nowell	179
St Columba	144	*Theodoric*	*124*
St Denio	145	This joyful Eastertide	
St Edmund	146	(Vruechten)	180
St Flavian	147	Thornbury	181
St Francis Xavier	148	Truro	182
St Fulbert	149	University	183
St George's Windsor	150	University College	184
St Helen	151	*Unser Herrscher*	*110*
St John Damascene	152	Veni Emmanuel	185
St Magnus	153	Veni Sancte Spiritus	186
St Matthew	154	Victory	187
St Peter	155	*Vruechten*	*180*
St Stephen	156	*Vulpius*	*59*
St Theodulph	157	Wareham	188
St Thomas (Webbe)	158	Was lebet	189
Salzburg (Hintze)	159	Were you there	190
Sandys	160	Westminster	191
Savannah	161	Westminster Abbey	192
Shipston	162	Wiltshire	193
Sing hosanna	163	Winchester New	194
Slane	164	Winchester Old	195
Somervell	165	Wir pflügen	196
Song 1	166	Wolvercote	197
Song 22	167	Woodlands	198
Song 34 (Angels' Song)	168	Württemberg	199
Southwell (Damon)	169	Yorkshire (Stockport)	200
Stille Nacht	170		
Stockport	*200*		
Stockton	171		
Stracathro	172		
Strength and stay	173		
Stuttgart	174		

1 ABBOT'S LEIGH

Cyril Vincent Taylor (1907-1991)

Key of C

© Copyright Oxford University Press. Used by permission.

Key of D

2 ABERYSTWYTH

Joseph Parry (1841-1903)

Key of D minor

Key of E minor

© Copyright 1998 Kevin Mayhew Ltd.

3 ABRIDGE

Isaac Smith (1734-1805)

Key of C

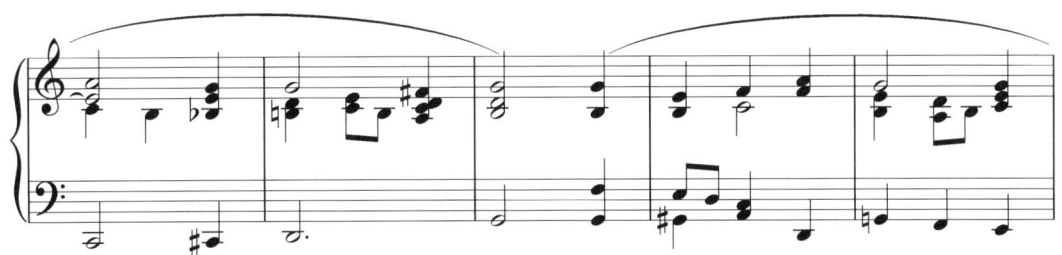

See over for another key

© Copyright 1998 Kevin Mayhew Ltd.

Key of D

4 ADESTE FIDELES

Attributed to John Francis Wade (1711-1786)

© Copyright 1998 Kevin Mayhew Ltd.

5 ALL FOR JESUS

John Stainer (1840-1901)

Key of C

Key of D

© Copyright 1998 Kevin Mayhew Ltd.

6 ALL SAINTS

From 'Geistreiches Gesangbuch', Darmstadt (1698)
adapted by William Henry Monk (1823-1889)

Key of B♭

Key of C

© Copyright 1998 Kevin Mayhew Ltd.

7 ALL THINGS BRIGHT AND BEAUTIFUL

William Henry Monk (1823-1889)

© Copyright 1998 Kevin Mayhew Ltd.

8 AMEN COURT

John Dykes Bower (1905-1981)

Key of F

© Copyright Hymns Ancient & Modern Ltd. Used by permission.

See over for another key

Key of G

© Copyright Hymns Ancient & Modern Ltd. Used by permission.

9 ANGEL VOICES

Edwin George Monk (1819-1900)

© Copyright 1998 Kevin Mayhew Ltd.

10 ANIMA CHRISTI

William Joseph Maher (1823-1877)

Key of F

See over for another key

Key of G

11 AR HYD Y NOS

Traditional Welsh melody

Key of F

12 AURELIA

Samuel Sebastian Wesley (1810-1876)

13 AUS DER TIEFE (HEINLEIN)

From 'Nürnbergisches Gesangbuch'
(1676)

© Copyright 2006 Kevin Mayhew Ltd.

14 AUSTRIA

Croatian folk melody adapted by
Franz Joseph Haydn (1732-1809)

© Copyright 1998 Kevin Mayhew Ltd.

15 AVE VIRGO VIRGINUM

As set in Johannes Leisentritt's 'Catholicum Hymnologium Germanicum', Cologne (1584)

16 BILLING

Richard Runciman Terry (1865-1938)

Key of D

See over for another key

© Copyright 1998 Kevin Mayhew Ltd.

17 BINCHESTER
William Croft (1678-1727)

© Copyright 1998 Kevin Mayhew Ltd.

Key of G

18 BISHOPTHORPE
Probably by Jeremiah Clarke (c.1674-1707)

© Copyright 1998 Kevin Mayhew Ltd.

19 BLAENWERN

William Penfro Rowlands (1860-1937)

Key of F

Key of G

20 BOW BRICKHILL

Sydney Hugo Nicholson (1875-1947)

21 BRISTOL

Thomas Ravenscroft (c.1582-c.1633)

Key of F

Key of G

22 BROTHER JAMES' AIR

Brother James Leith Macbeth Bain (1860-1925)

© Copyright 1998 Kevin Mayhew Ltd.

23 BUCKLAND

Leighton George Hayne (1836-1883)

Key of C

Key of D

© Copyright 1998 Kevin Mayhew Ltd.

24 BUNESSAN

Traditional Gaelic melody

25 CAITHNESS

From the 'Scottish Psalter' (1635)

Key of C

Key of D

Key of E♭

© Copyright 1998 Kevin Mayhew Ltd.

26 CAPETOWN

Friedrich Filitz (1804-1876)

Key of C

Key of D

© Copyright 1998 Kevin Mayhew Ltd.

27 CARLISLE

Charles Lockhart (1745-1815)

28 CASWALL

Friedrich Filitz (1804-1876)

29 CONTEMPLATION

Frederick Arthur Gore Ouseley (1825-1889)

30 CRADLE SONG (AWAY IN A MANGER)

William James Kirkpatrick (1838-1921)

31 CRANHAM

Gustav Holst (1874-1934)

© Copyright 1998 Kevin Mayhew Ltd.

32 CRIMOND

Jessie Seymour Irvine (1836-1887)

33 CROFT'S 136TH

William Croft (1678-1727)

© Copyright 1998 Kevin Mayhew Ltd.

34 CROSS OF JESUS

John Stainer (1840-1901)

35 CRÜGER

From Johann Crüger's 'Gesangbuch' adapted by
William Henry Monk (1823-1889)

Key of E♭

Key of F

36 CULBACH

Adapted from a chorale in J. Scheffler's 'Heilige Seelenlust', Breslau (1657)

© Copyright 1998 Kevin Mayhew Ltd.

37 CWM RHONDDA

John Hughes (1873-1932)

38 DARWALL'S 148TH

John Darwall (1731-1789)

© Copyright 1998 Kevin Mayhew Ltd.

39 DEUS, TUORUM MILITUM

From 'Grenoble Antiphoner' (1753)

40 DIADEMATA

George Job Elvey (1816-1893)

Key of C

See over for another key

Key of D

41 DIX

Adapted from Conrad Kocher (1786-1872)
by William Henry Monk (1823-1889)

© Copyright 1998 Kevin Mayhew Ltd.

42 DOMINUS REGIT ME

John Bacchus Dykes (1823-1876)

Key of F

Key of G

© Copyright 1998 Kevin Mayhew Ltd.

43 DOWN AMPNEY

Ralph Vaughan Williams (1872-1958)

44 DUKE STREET

Attributed to John Hatton (d.1793)

Key of C

Key of D

© Copyright 1998 Kevin Mayhew Ltd.

45 DUNDEE

From the 'Scottish Psalter', Edinburgh (1615)

46 EASTER HYMN

From 'Lyra Davidica' (1708)

Key of B♭

See over for another key

© Copyright 1998 Kevin Mayhew Ltd.

Key of C

47 EIN' FESTE BURG

Martin Luther (1483-1546)

Key of C

See over for another key

Key of D

48 EISENACH (MACH'S MIT MIR GOTT)

Johann Hermann Schein (1586-1630)
in his revised 'Cantional' (1645)

© Copyright 1998 Kevin Mayhew Ltd.

49 ELLACOMBE

From 'Württemberg Gesangbuch' (1784)

Key of G

Key of A

© Copyright 1998 Kevin Mayhew Ltd.

Key of B♭

50 ELLERS

Edward John Hopkins (1818-1901)

Key of A♭

51 ES IST EIN' ROS' ENTSPRUNGEN

German Carol melody

52 EVELYNS

William Henry Monk (1823-1889)

Key of D

© Copyright 1998 Kevin Mayhew Ltd.

Key of E♭

53 EVENTIDE

William Henry Monk (1823-1889)

54 EWING

Alexander Ewing (1830-1895)

Key of C

Key of D

55 FARLEY CASTLE

Henry Lawes (1596-1662)

© Copyright 1998 Kevin Mayhew Ltd.

56 FOREST GREEN

Traditional English melody collected by
Ralph Vaughan Williams (1872-1958)

© Copyright Oxford University Press. Used by permission.

57 FRANCONIA

From 'Harmonischer Liederschatz' (1738)
adapted by William Henry Havergal (1793-1870)

Key of C

Key of D

58 FULDA

From William Gardiner's 'Sacred Melodies' (1815)

© Copyright 1998 Kevin Mayhew Ltd.

59 GELOB'T SEI GOTT (VULPIUS)

From Melchior Vulpius' 'Gesangbuch' (1609)

60 GERONTIUS

John Bacchus Dykes (1823-1876)

© Copyright 1998 Kevin Mayhew Ltd.

61 GOD REST YOU MERRY

Traditional English melody

Key of D minor

Key of E minor

© Copyright 1998 Kevin Mayhew Ltd.

62 GONFALON ROYAL

Percy Carter Buck (1871-1947)

A - - men.

63 GOPSAL

George Frideric Handel (1685-1759)

© Copyright 1998 Kevin Mayhew Ltd.

64 GREENSLEEVES

Traditional English melody

65 GWALCHMAI

Joseph David Jones (1827-1870)

66 HANOVER

William Croft (1678-1727)

67 HAREWOOD

Samuel Sebastian Wesley (1810-1876)

Key of F

© Copyright 1998 Kevin Mayhew Ltd.　　*See over for another two keys*

68 HELMSLEY

From John Wesley's 'Select Hymns with Tunes Annext' (1765)

69 HEREFORD

Samuel Sebastian Wesley (1810-1876)

Key of E

© Copyright 1998 Kevin Mayhew Ltd.

70 HERONGATE

Traditional English melody collected by
Ralph Vaughan Williams (1872-1958)

Key of D

See over for another key

© Copyright Oxford University Press. Used by permission.

Key of E♭

71 HIGHWOOD

Richard Runciman Terry (1865-1938)

72 HOLLINGSIDE

John Bacchus Dykes (1823-1876)

Key of D

See over for another key

Key of E♭

73 HORSLEY

William Horsley (1774-1858)

Key of D

Key of E♭

© Copyright 1998 Kevin Mayhew Ltd.

74 HYFRYDOL

Rowland Huw Pritchard (1811-1887)

75 IRBY

Henry John Gauntlett (1805-1876)

76 IRISH

From 'Hymns and Sacred Poems',
Dublin (1749)

77 KILMARNOCK

Neil Dougall (1776-1862)

© Copyright 1998 Kevin Mayhew Ltd.

78 KING'S LYNN

Traditional English melody

Key of C minor

Key of D minor

© Copyright 1998 Kevin Mayhew Ltd.

79 KINGSFOLD

Traditional English melody

80 LASST UNS ERFREUEN

From 'Geistliche Kirchengesäng',
Cologne (1623)

Key of D

Key of E♭

81 LAUDATE DOMINUM

Charles Hubert Hastings Parry (1848-1918)

82 LAUDES DOMINI

Joseph Barnby (1838-1896)

83 LAUS DEO (REDHEAD NO. 46)

Richard Redhead (1820-1901)

84 LEONI

Traditional Hebrew melody

Key of E minor

Key of F minor

85 LITTLE CORNARD

Martin Shaw (1875-1958)

Key of B minor

Key of C minor

© Copyright The Martin Shaw Trust. Exclusively licensed to
and reproduced by kind permission of J. Curwen & Sons Ltd.

86 LLANFAIR

Robert Williams (1781-1821)

Key of F

See over for another key

87 LOBE DEN HERREN

From 'Praxis Pietatis Melica' (1668)

Key of F

See over for another key

88 LOVE DIVINE

John Stainer (1840-1901)

Key of G

© Copyright 1998 Kevin Mayhew Ltd.

89 LOVE UNKNOWN

John Ireland (1879-1962)

Key of C

See over for another two keys

© Copyright The John Ireland Trust. Used by permission.

Key of D

Key of E♭

90 LUCKINGTON

Basil Harwood (1859-1949)

Key of C

See over for another key

© Copyright The Estate of Dr. Basil Harwood. Reproduced by kind permission
of the Trustees of the late Dr. Basil Harwood Settlement Trust.

© Copyright The Estate of Dr. Basil Harwood. Reproduced by kind permission
of the Trustees of the late Dr. Basil Harwood Settlement Trust.

91 LUX EOI

Arthur Seymour Sullivan (1842-1900)

© Copyright 1998 Kevin Mayhew Ltd.

Key of C

92 MACCABAEUS

George Frideric Handel (1685-1759)

Key of D

Key of E♭

93 MANNHEIM

Friedrich Filitz (1804-1876)

Key of D

Key of E♭

Key of E

94 MARCHING

Martin Shaw (1875-1958)

Key of F

© Copyright 1998 Kevin Mayhew Ltd.

See over for another two keys

© Copyright The Martin Shaw Trust. Exclusively licensed to
and reproduced by kind permission of J. Curwen & Sons Ltd.

Key of G

Key of A

95 MARTYRDOM

Hugh Wilson (1766-1824)

© Copyright 1998 Kevin Mayhew Ltd.

96 MELCOMBE

Samuel Webbe (1740-1816)

97 MELITA

John Bacchus Dykes (1823-1876)

98 MENDELSSOHN

Adapted from Felix Mendelssohn (1809-1847)
by William Hayman Cummings (1831-1915)

Key of F

© Copyright 1998 Kevin Mayhew Ltd.

Key of G

99 MERTON

William Henry Monk (1823-1889)

100 MICHAEL

Herbert Howells (1892-1983)

© Copyright 1968 Novello & Co. Ltd. Used by permission.

101 MILES LANE

William Shrubsole (1760-1806)

Key of A

102 MONKLAND

From 'Hymn Tunes of the United Brethren'
adapted by John Bernard Wilkes (1785-1869)

© Copyright 1998 Kevin Mayhew Ltd.

103 MONKS GATE

Traditional English melody
collected by Ralph Vaughan Williams (1872-1958)

Key of D

© Copyright Oxford University Press. Used by permission.

Key of E♭

104 MORNING HYMN

François Hippolyte Barthélémon (1741-1808)

© Copyright Oxford University Press. Used by permission.

© Copyright 1998 Kevin Mayhew Ltd.

105 MORNING LIGHT

George James Webb (1803-1887)

Key of G

Key of A

© Copyright 1998 Kevin Mayhew Ltd.

106 MOSCOW

From Madan's 'Collection' (1769)
adapted by Felice de Giardini (1716-1796)

107 MOUNT EPHRAIM

Benjamin Milgrove (1731-1810)

Key of C

Key of D

108 NARENZA

From Johannes Leisentritt's
'Catholicum Hymnologium Germanicum' Cologne (1584)
adapted by William Henry Havergal (1793-1870)

Key of A

Key of B♭

109 NATIVITY

Henry Lahee (1836-1912)

© Copyright 1998 Kevin Mayhew Ltd.

110 NEANDER (UNSER HERRSCHER)

Joachim Neander (1650-1680)

111 NICAEA

John Bacchus Dykes (1823-1876)

© Copyright 1998 Kevin Mayhew Ltd.

112 NOEL

Traditional English melody
adapted by Arthur Seymour Sullivan (1842-1900)

113 NOEL NOUVELET

Traditional French melody

Key of E minor

© Copyright 1998 Kevin Mayhew Ltd.

Key of F minor

114 NUN DANKET

Johann Crüger (1598-1662)

Key of E♭

See over for another key

© Copyright 1998 Kevin Mayhew Ltd.

Key of F

115 OBIIT   Walter Parratt (1841-1924)

© Copyright 1998 Kevin Mayhew Ltd.

116 OFFERTORIUM

Adapted from Michael Haydn (1737-1806)

Key of C

See over for another key

© Copyright 1998 Kevin Mayhew Ltd.

Key of D

117 O FILII ET FILIAE

From 'Airs sur les hymnes sacres', Paris (1683)

VERSION A

© Copyright 1998 Kevin Mayhew Ltd.

VERSION B

118 OLD 100TH

'Genevan Psalter' (1551), attributed to Louis Bourgeois (c.1510-c.1561)

119 OLD 104TH

Thomas Ravenscroft's 'Psalms' (1621)

© Copyright 1998 Kevin Mayhew Ltd.

120 OLD 120TH

From Thomas Este's 'Psalter' (1592)

121 ORIEL

Caspar Ett's 'Cantica Sacra' (1840)

© Copyright 1998 Kevin Mayhew Ltd.

122 PADERBORN

From the 'Paderborn Gesangbuch' (1765)

Key of F

Key of G

© Copyright 1998 Kevin Mayhew Ltd.

123 PASSION CHORALE

Hans Leo Hassler (1564-1612)

124 PERSONENT HODIE (THEODORIC)

Key of D minor

From 'Piae Cantiones' (1582)

Key of E minor

125 PETRA (REDHEAD NO. 76)

Richard Redhead (1820-1901)

© Copyright 1998 Kevin Mayhew Ltd.

126 PICARDY

French carol melody in 'Chansons Populaires'
Vol. 4, Paris (1860)

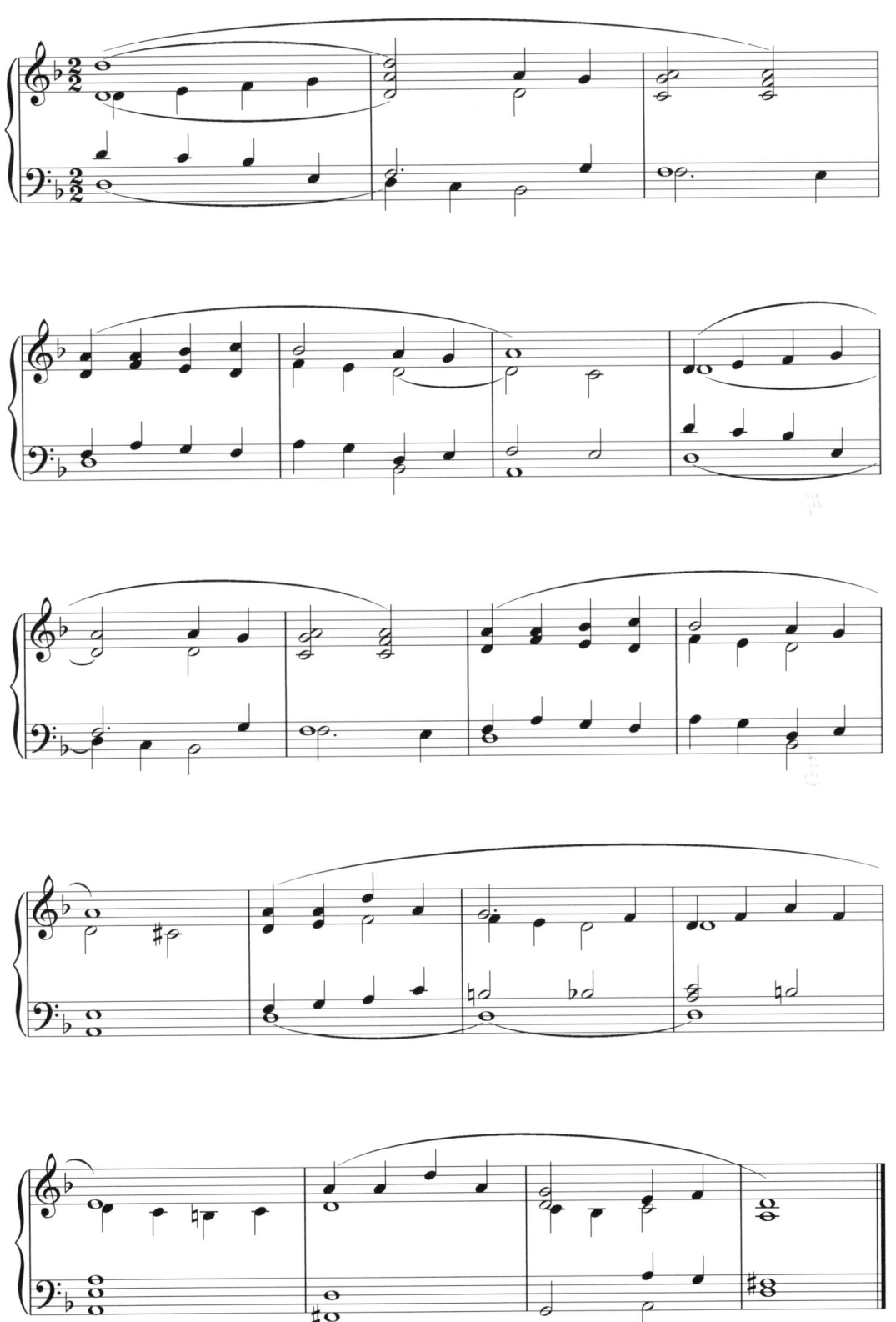

127 PRAISE, MY SOUL

John Goss (1800-1880)

128 PUER NOBIS NASCITUR

Adapted by Michael Praetorius (1571-1621)

Key of C

© Copyright 1998 Kevin Mayhew Ltd.

Key of D

129 QUAM DILECTA

Henry Lascelles Jenner (1820-1898)

© Copyright 1998 Kevin Mayhew Ltd.

130 QUEM PASTORES

German carol melody (14th century)

131 RATISBON

From Johann Gottlob Werner's 'Choralbuch' Leipzig (1815)

132 RAVENSHAW

From M. Weisse's 'Ein neu Gesangbüchlein'
adapted by William Henry Monk (1823-1889)

133 REGENT SQUARE

Henry Smart (1813-1879)

134 REPTON

Charles Hubert Hastings Parry (1848-1918)

135 REX GLORIAE

Henry Smart (1813-1879)

Key of G

See over for another key

© Copyright 1998 Kevin Mayhew Ltd.

Key of A♭

136 RHUDDLAN

Traditional Welsh melody from
'Musical Relicks of Welsh Bards' (1800)

137 RICHMOND

Adapted from Thomas Haweis (1734-1820)

Key of E♭

See over for another two keys

© Copyright 1998 Kevin Mayhew Ltd.

Key of F

Key of G

138 ROCKINGHAM

From A. Williams' 'Second Supplement to Psalmody in Miniature' (c.1780)
adapted by Edward Miller (1735-1807)

139 ROYAL OAK

Traditional English melody adapted by Martin Shaw (1875-1958)

© Copyright Oxford University Press. Used by permission.

Key of A♭

140 SAFFRON WALDEN

Arthur Henry Brown (1830-1926)

141 ST ANNE

William Croft (1678-1727)

142 ST BERNARD

Adapted from a melody in 'Tochter Sion' (1741)

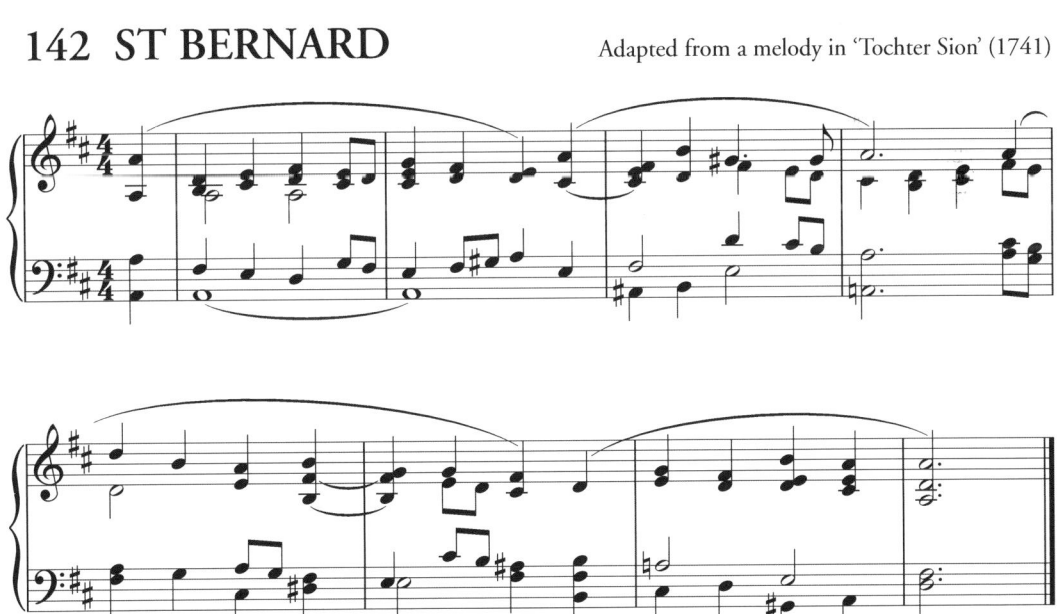

© Copyright 1998 Kevin Mayhew Ltd.

143 ST CLEMENT

Clement Cotterill Scholefield (1839-1904)

© Copyright 1998 Kevin Mayhew Ltd.

144 ST COLUMBA

Irish melody from 'The Complete Petrie Collection of Ancient Irish Music' (1855) ed. Charles Villiers Stanford (1902)

© Copyright 1998 Kevin Mayhew Ltd.

145 ST DENIO

Adapted from a traditional Welsh hymn melody
in John Roberts' 'Caniadau y Cysegr' (1839)

146 ST EDMUND

Charles Steggall (1826-1905)

Key of F

See over for another key

© Copyright 1998 Kevin Mayhew Ltd.

Key of G

147 ST FLAVIAN

From Day's 'Psalter' (1562)

148 ST FRANCIS XAVIER

John Stainer (1840-1901)

© Copyright 1998 Kevin Mayhew Ltd.

149 ST FULBERT

Henry John Gauntlett (1805-1876)

Key of D

Key of E♭

150 ST GEORGE'S WINDSOR

George Job Elvey (1816-1893)

Key of E♭

Key of F

151 ST HELEN

George Clement Martin (1844-1916)

152 ST JOHN DAMASCENE

Arthur Henry Brown (1830-1926)

Key of F

Key of G

153 ST MAGNUS

Jeremiah Clarke (1670-1707)

154 ST MATTHEW

William Croft (1678-1727)

156 ST STEPHEN

William Jones (1726-1800)

VERSION B
Key of B♭

© Copyright 1998 Kevin Mayhew Ltd.

See over for another key

Key of C

158 ST THOMAS (WEBBE)

Samuel Webbe (1740-1816)

© Copyright 1998 Kevin Mayhew Ltd.

159 SALZBURG (HINTZE)

Jacob Hintze (1622-1702)

Key of C

Key of D

160 SANDYS

Traditional English carol
from William Sandys' 'Christmas Carols' (1833)

161 SAVANNAH

From Herrnhut collection (c.1740)
in John Wesley's 'Foundery Collection' (1742)

162 SHIPSTON
Warwickshire ballad

Key of D

Key of E♭

163 SING HOSANNA
Traditional melody

Key of D

© Copyright 1998 Kevin Mayhew Ltd.

Key of E♭

164 SLANE

Traditional Irish melody

165 SOMERVELL

Arthur Somervell (1863-1937)

166 SONG 1

Orlando Gibbons (1583-1625)

© Copyright 1998 Kevin Mayhew Ltd.

167 SONG 22

Orlando Gibbons (1583-1625)

168 SONG 34 (ANGELS' SONG)

Orlando Gibbons (1583-1625)

© Copyright 1998 Kevin Mayhew Ltd.

169 SOUTHWELL (DAMON)

From 'The Psalmes in English Meter' (1579)
adapted by William Damon (1540-1591)

© Copyright 1998 Kevin Mayhew Ltd.

Key of E minor

170 STILLE NACHT

Franz Xaver Grüber (1787-1863)

© Copyright 1998 Kevin Mayhew Ltd.

171 STOCKTON
Thomas Wright (1763-1829)

Key of C

Key of D

172 STRACATHRO
Charles Hutcheson (1792-1860)

© Copyright 1998 Kevin Mayhew Ltd.

173 STRENGTH AND STAY

John Bacchus Dykes (1823-1876)

© Copyright 1998 Kevin Mayhew Ltd.

174 STUTTGART

German melody

175 SURREY

Henry Carey (c.1690-1743)

Key of E♭

See over for another key

© Copyright 1998 Kevin Mayhew Ltd.

Key of F

176 SUSSEX CAROL

**Traditional English melody
collected by Ralph Vaughan Williams (1872-1958)**

© Copyright 1919 Stainer & Bell Ltd. Used by permission.

177 TALLIS' CANON

Thomas Tallis (c.1505-1585)

Key of F

© Copyright 1998 Kevin Mayhew Ltd.

See over for another key

178 TALLIS' ORDINAL

Thomas Tallis (c.1505-1585)

179 THE FIRST NOWELL

Traditional English melody

© Copyright 1998 Kevin Mayhew Ltd.

180 THIS JOYFUL EASTERTIDE
(VRUECHTEN)

Traditional Dutch melody

Key of E♭

Key of F

181 THORNBURY

Basil Harwood (1859-1949)

Key of C

© Copyright the Executors of Dr. Basil Harwood. Used by permission of the Trustees of the late Dr Basil Harwood Settlement Trust.

Key of D

© Copyright the Executors of Dr. Basil Harwood. Used by permission of the Trustees of the late Dr Basil Harwood Settlement Trust.

182 TRURO

From Thomas Williams'
'Psalmodia Evangelica' (1789)

Key of C

Key of D

© Copyright 1998 Kevin Mayhew Ltd.

183 UNIVERSITY
Charles Collignon (1725-1785)

Key of B♭

Key of C

184 UNIVERSITY COLLEGE
Henry John Gauntlett (1805-1876)

Key of E♭

See over for another key

© Copyright 1998 Kevin Mayhew Ltd.

Key of F

185 VENI EMMANUEL

Adapted by Thomas Helmore (1811-1890)
from a French Missal

Key of D minor

© Copyright 1998 Kevin Mayhew Ltd.

Key of E minor

186 VENI SANCTE SPIRITUS

Samuel Webbe (1740-1816)

187 VICTORY

Giovanni Pierluigi da Palestrina (c.1525-1594)
adapted by William Henry Monk (1823-1889)

© Copyright 1998 Kevin Mayhew Ltd.

188 WAREHAM

William Knapp (1698-1768)

189 WAS LEBET

From the 'Rheinhardt' MS, Üttingen (1754)

190 WERE YOU THERE

Spiritual

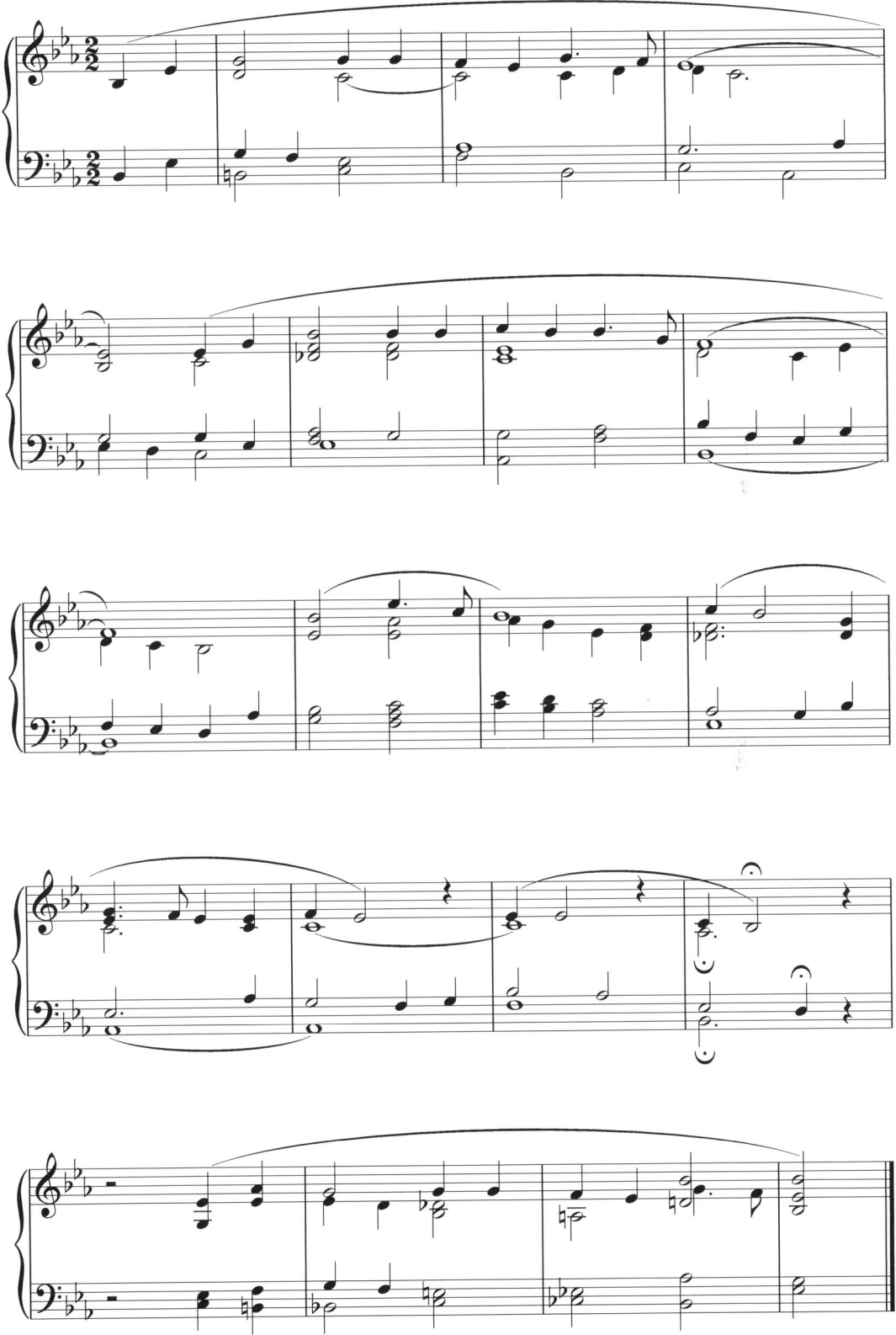

© Copyright 1998 Kevin Mayhew Ltd.

191 WESTMINSTER

James Turle (1802-1882)

192 WESTMINSTER ABBEY

Henry Purcell (1659-1695)

Key of F

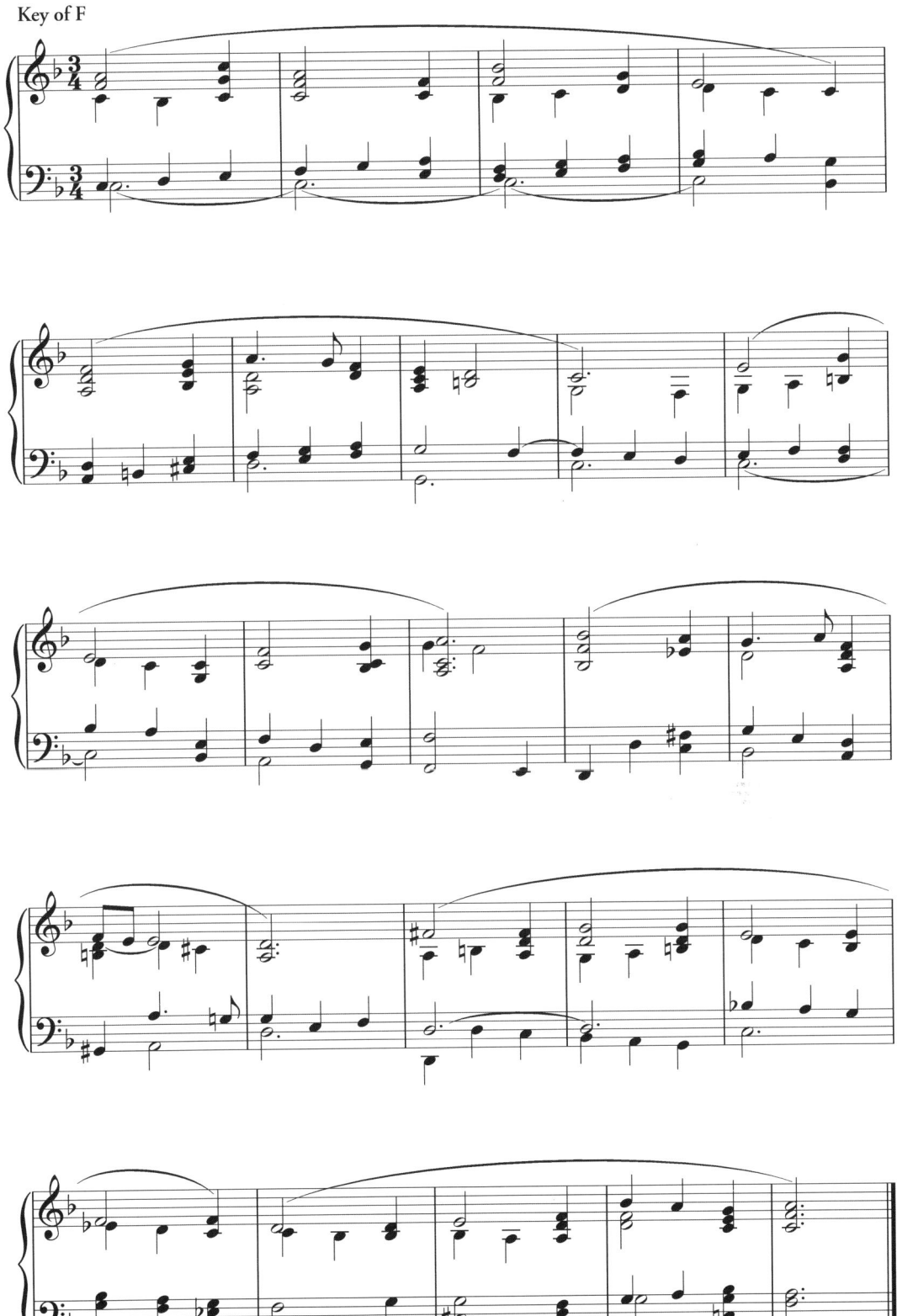

See over for another two keys

© Copyright 1998 Kevin Mayhew Ltd.

Key of G

Key of A

193 WILTSHIRE

George Thomas Smart (1776-1867)

VERSION A
Key of G

VERSION B
Key of A

Key of B♭

194 WINCHESTER NEW

From 'Musikalisches Handbuch' (1690)

195 WINCHESTER OLD

From Este's 'Psalter' (1592)

196 WIR PFLÜGEN

Johann Abraham Peter Schulz (1747-1800)

Key of A♭

© Copyright 1998 Kevin Mayhew Ltd.

See over for another key

Key of A

197 WOLVERCOTE

William Harold Ferguson (1874-1950)

© Copyright Oxford University Press. Used by permission.

198 WOODLANDS

Walter Greatorex (1877-1949)

199 WÜRTTEMBERG

From 'Hundert Arien', Dresden (1694)

200 YORKSHIRE (STOCKPORT)

John Wainwright (1723-1768)

Key of B♭

Key of C